Jonah
The Reluctant Prophet

Also by Donna Lewis

CHOICES

PEPPI PUFFIN TO THE RESCUE

TIME TO FLY

EARTH, GOD'S GARDEN

Jonah
The Reluctant Prophet

by **Donna Lewis**
Illustrated by
Rebecca Bibbey

William R. Parks
Stanwrite@aol.com

www.wrparks.com

Jonah leaned back with a contented sigh.
He decided to sleep and let the day go by.
All was quiet, there was not even a peep
of a bird to disturb his afternoon sleep.

Then, "Jonah!" came
   a voice loud and clear.
Jonah sat up and
   trembled with fear.
"Jonah, hear me. This
   is God speaking to you!"
(Be honest, now, wouldn't
   that scare you, too?)

Jonah looked around,
   he saw no one close by.
"Maybe a dream," he thought,
   and closed one eye.
Again came the voice;
   Jonah raised up on his knees.
He looked all around
   through the surrounding trees.

He wanted to find a safe place to hide.
He wasn't just scared, he was terrified.
Jonah jumped to his feet and ran to his house.
Down to the cellar he crept, quiet as a mouse.

"Jonah," God said again, "Come and listen to me.
You are the one I want to see."
Jonah put both hands over his ears,
fell on his face, and gave way to his fears.

His whole body trembled and shook.
His voice croaked, "Yes, Lord?" He was afraid to look.
He really did not want to see.
"Why do you call? What can you want with me?"

God said, "Jonah, I have a job for you.
Nineveh is a wicked city. The people are evil and cruel, too.
To see them like that makes me very sad.
I want them to change, to be happy and glad."

"I need a messenger, someone to go there,
tell them I love them. Tell them I care.
You, Jonah, must go. It will be time well spent.
Tell everyone there that they must repent."

"What do I care?" Jonah mumbled.
 "Let them all perish," he grumbled.
"Let God send someone else to face that mob.
 Send someone better to do such a job."

I know how God works. No matter who is sent,
those people will listen and they will repent.
Then God will be kind and he will forgive.
That's what will happen, as sure as I live.

God said, "Tell them in forty days Nineveh will fall.
I will destroy people, animals, buildings and all."

Jonah decided, "I won't go. God can just send
someone else. Let Nineveh come to its bad end.
I'll go where no one can find me;
far away across the deep sea."

He slung a bag over his shoulder
and sneaked out of the house, feeling bolder.
He ran down the street, across the court,
out of town to the nearest seaport.

"To Tarshish I'll go, no one can find me there."
Foolish Jonah, didn't he know God is everywhere?
Down in the hold of the ship he crept,
and there, tired out, at last he slept.

While Jonah rested, God sent strong winds that blew
a terrible storm, so bad that even the crew
thought the ship would go down.
If they sank, everyone on board would drown.

The captain knew someone on the ship was to blame.
Just then Jonah awoke. Out of the hold he came.
"I am the one," he said. "Throw me into the sea.
This storm is sent because of me."

Over the rail he was swept by a great wave.
Jonah was scared, but he tried to be brave.

Instantly the storm stopped. The dashing waves became calm.
The sailors praised God and sang a thankful psalm.

But what of Jonah? Did he drown?
He did sink; he went down, down, down.

Deep in the water he made a prayful wish,
and before he hit bottom, along came a fish.
The biggest fish you ever could think,
and it swallowed Jonah as quick as a wink.

"Oh God, help me, get me out of here! I'll do whatever you ask.
I'll go to Nineveh and do that unpleasant task."
For three long days and long nights Jonah prayed and moaned.
All that time, he prayed and groaned.

That fish, too, was not happy; its stomach was sore.
And finally after three days, it spit Jonah out onto the shore.

And Jonah prayed.
 "Oh, God, thank you, Lord, God of all creation.
Thank you for my deliverance and salvation."

"When you called and I fled from your sight,
I hid from you, but in the midst of my flight,
when into the depths of the ocean I was hurled,
down in deep water to the floor of the world,
 when all hope was gone, I faced death and despair,
God, our living God, was with me there."

So on to Nineveh Jonah went.
     He did as God said.
He learned to follow,
     and went where God led.

He told the people they must change their wicked ways
Or God would destroy their whole city in just forty days.

Every day on corners and in the market place
he told the people face to face.
"Repent and change your wicked way,
turn back to God. Listen and obey."

And they did. They prayed God would forgive.
"God is merciful. He will let us live."

And lo!
The forty days passed. God looked down with pity.
He forgave and saved their fair city.
Everyone in Nineveh was filled with great joy.
Every woman and man, every girl and boy.

But what of Jonah? Did he laugh? Did he shout?
No, he went off by himself to sulk and to pout.

"I knew, God, what you would do.
That's why I ran and hid from you.
I preached everywhere of distruction and fire;
now they all think I'm nothing but a liar.
Why didn't you leave me alone?
I knew they would listen and they would atone.
They were sorry and now you will win.
You always forgive and forget every sin."

"Oh, Jonah, are you such a selfish soul?
Shouldn't rescuing everyone be my ultimate goal?
I am with you, my prophet, always with you.
Don't you want me to be with all my people, too?
Would you be happy to have everyone lost?
Just to prove you were right, at such a great cost?"

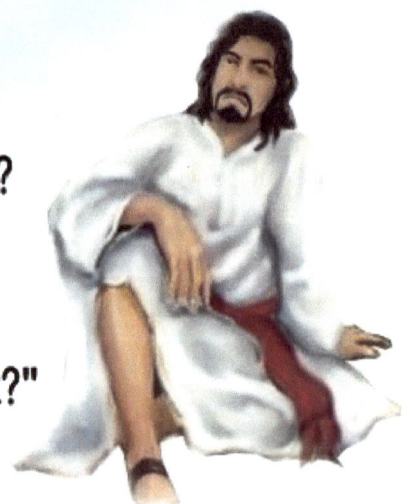

"Jonah, did you make the earth,
the heavens, all things of great worth?
I love my creation, every soul and heart,
be happy, Jonah, for doing your part.

Does not your name mean 'dove'?
A dove of peace to bring God's message of love.
Rejoice always for every saved soul.
God's final aim is for all to be made whole."

Peace

Handbook for Piano Practice

Colours of Fire

Letters to a Young Math Teacher

Letters from John Dewey/Letters from Huck Finn

Program Your Calculator

A Franciscan Odyssey

The Nature Watch Collection Book One

The Nature Watch Collection Book Two

Boolean Algebra and Switching Circuits

Computer Number Bases

Political Economics

Economic History

Peppin Puffin to the Rescue

Choices

Time to Fly

Earth, God's Garden